LG-2.1-0.5

4/15

Animal COLORS

What They Mean

by J. Clark Sawyer

Consultants:
Christopher Kuhar, PhD
Executive Director, Cleveland Metroparks Zoo
Cleveland, Ohio

Kimberly Brenneman, PhD
National Institute for Early Education Research, Rutgers University
New Brunswick, New Jersey

BEARPORT
PUBLISHING

New York, New York

Credits

TOC, © Thinkstock; 4, © Shutterstock; 5, © Thinkstock; 6–7, © Steve Winter/National Geographic Creative; 8, © Bill Kennedy/Shutterstock; 9, © Jurgen Freund/Nature Picture Library/Corbis; 10–11, © Ken Koskela/Alamy; 12–13, © Mark Kostich/Getty Images; 14–15, © Shutterstock; 16, © Steven J. Kazlowski/Alamy; 17, © RGB Ventures LLC dba SuperStock/Alamy; 18, © Klaus Nigge/Getty Images; 19L, © Le Do/Shutterstock; 19R, © Atlaspix/Shutterstock; 20–21, © petervician/Thinkstock; 22A, © ODM/Shutterstock; 22B, © Nantawat Chotsuwan/Shutterstock; 22C, © Patrick K. Campbell/Shutterstock; 22D, © Matthias Breiter/Getty Images/Minden Pictures; 22E, © Eric Isselee/Shutterstock; 22F, © Yury Taranik/Thinkstock; 22G, © iStockphoto/Thinkstock; 22H, © littlesam/Shutterstock; 22I, © Shutterstock; 23TL, © iStockphoto/Thinkstock; 23TM, © iStockphoto/Thinkstock; 23TR, © iStockphoto/Thinkstock; 23BL, © Cuson/Shutterstock; 23BM, © iStockphoto/Thinkstock; 23BR, © yykkaa/Shutterstock; 24, © Eric Isselee/Shutterstock.

Publisher: Kenn Goin
Editor: Jessica Rudolph
Creative Director: Spencer Brinker
Design: Debrah Kaiser
Photo Researcher: Michael Win

Library of Congress Cataloging-in-Publication Data

Clark Sawyer, J., author.
  Animal colors : what they mean / by J. Clark Sawyer.
      pages cm.—(Colors tell a story)
  Includes bibliographical references and index.
  ISBN-13: 978-1-62724-321-6 (library binding)
  ISBN-10: 1-62724-321-6 (library binding)
  1. Animals—Color—Juvenile literature. 2. Camouflage (Biology)—Juvenile literature.
  3. Colors—Juvenile literature. I. Title.
  QL767.C554 2015
  591.47′2—dc23
                                        2014008474

For more information, write to Bearport Publishing Company, Inc., 45 West 21st Street, Suite 3B, New York, New York 10010. Printed in the United States of America.

10 9 8 7 6 5 4 3 2 1

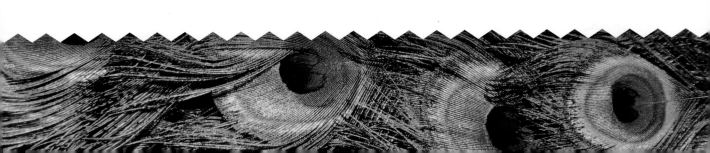

Contents

Animal Colors

Animals are many different colors.

Their colors often tell you something special about them.

Some colors help animals hide when they hunt.

A tiger blends in with grass.

Its **prey** can't see the animal's orange and black fur.

Colors can also help animals hide from **predators**.

Some sea horses are yellow or red.

They blend in with **coral** in the ocean.

9

Sometimes bright colors warn predators to stay away.

This blue frog is **poisonous**.

If an animal eats the frog, it may die.

A coral snake has yellow, black, and red bands.

These colors say, "Don't come near!"

The snake's poisonous bite can kill.

13

14

A ladybug is bright red with black spots.

Birds know not to eat it.

This **insect** tastes awful!

The colors of some animals change to help them hide when hunting.

The Arctic fox's fur is white during winter to blend in with snow.

It turns grayish brown in the summer to blend in with dirt and rocks.

Colors can change as animals grow up, too.

Flamingo chicks start out white.

They turn bright pink
as they grow.

Some animals use colors to attract a **mate**.

A male peacock shows off its blue and green feathers.

All around the world, animal colors tell a story!

Look at the animals below. They all use their colors to try to stay hidden in their environment. For each animal, choose the place where it would best blend in.

1. fish **2. snake** **3. Arctic hare** **4. lion**

A **B** **C** **D**

Answers are on page 24.

Glossary

coral (KOR-uhl) tiny sea creatures that form rock-like structures in shallow ocean water

insect (IN-sekt) a small animal that has six legs, three main body parts, two antennae, and a hard covering

mate (MAYT) a male or female partner

poisonous (POI-zuhn-uhss) having a substance that can harm or kill

predators (PRED-uh-turz) animals that hunt other animals for food

prey (PRAY) an animal that is hunted by other animals for food

Index

Read More

Fielding, Beth. *Animal Colors: A Rainbow of Colors from Animals Around the World.* Waynesville, NC: EarlyLight (2009).

Smith, Penny. *Animal Hide and Seek (DK Readers Level 1: Beginning to Read).* New York: DK (2006).

Learn More Online

To learn more about animal colors, visit
www.bearportpublishing.com/ColorsTellaStory

About the Author

J. Clark Sawyer lives in Connecticut. She has edited and written many books about history, science, and nature for children.

Answers for Page 22:

1. C; 2. D; 3. A; 4. B